# Table of Contents

I. Introduction

II. Creating Job Ads that Attract Gen Z

III. Attracting Gen Z Candidates

IV. Selecting Gen Z Candidates

V. Interview Guide for Hiring Gen Z

VI. Making Job Offers to Gen Z

VII. Case Studies and Examples of hiring Gen z candidates

VIII. Conclusion

References

# I. Introduction

So, you wanna know about Gen Z in the workplace, huh? Well, let me tell you, these youngsters are a pretty unique bunch! They were born in the late 90s and early 2000s, so they've grown up in a world of rapid change and technological advancements.

One of the big things about Gen Z is that they're incredibly tech-savvy. They've grown up with smartphones, social media, and all sorts of other digital tools, so they're super comfortable using them in the workplace. They're always looking for new and innovative ways to use technology to improve productivity and make work more efficient. Another thing that sets Gen Z apart is their desire for work-life balance. They're not interested in working 80-hour weeks or sacrificing their personal lives for the sake of their careers. They value flexibility and freedom, and they want to be able to work from anywhere, anytime.

But don't let that fool you into thinking that they're lazy or unmotivated. In fact, Gen Z is incredibly driven and ambitious. They're not content to just sit back and watch the world go by - they want to make a difference and have a positive impact on society. Gen Z is a very diverse generation. They come from all sorts of different backgrounds and have a wide range of experiences and perspectives. This makes them incredibly creative and innovative, and it also means that they value inclusivity and diversity in the workplace. They want to work in environments that celebrate differences and encourage collaboration and cooperation.

However, recruiting Gen Z can also be challenging because they have different expectations and preferences than previous generations. Gen Z is highly tech-savvy and prefers digital communication channels, such as texting and social media, over traditional methods like email or phone calls. They are also more socially and environmentally conscious than previous generations, and they prioritize work-life balance, career growth opportunities, and meaningful work. Therefore, companies need to adapt their recruitment strategies to appeal to Gen Z candidates. This may include utilizing social media platforms for recruitment, showcasing the company's values and commitment to social responsibility, providing flexible work arrangements, and offering opportunities for learning and career development. Companies that fail to adapt to Gen Z's preferences and values risk missing out on top talent and may struggle to retain their younger employees. But fear not, because in this eBook, we'll provide you with a comprehensive guide on how to attract, select, and hire the best Gen Z candidates for your organization.

We'll cover everything from creating job ads that speak to Gen Z, to designing structured interview processes, to making compelling job offers. We'll also include case studies and examples of companies that have effectively hired and retained Gen Z employees.

## I.1. Gen Z: why they are important in the workforce.

Picture 1.1. Infographic: 3 Key Gen Z Statistic You Must Know

Gen Z is the generation born between 1997 and 2012, making them currently between the ages of 9 and 24, as well as the youngest generation in the workforce today. They are digital natives who grew up with technology and have a unique set of skills and perspectives that set them apart from previous generations. This generation is an important addition to the workforce because they bring fresh ideas and a willingness to challenge the status quo. They are highly adaptable and thrive in fast-paced environments that require quick thinking and problem-solving skills. They also value work-life balance, diversity and inclusion, and social responsibility. As the baby boomer generation retires and the millennial generation moves into leadership roles, Gen Z is poised to become the largest generation in the workforce. Employers who understand how to attract, retain, and develop Gen Z talent will have a competitive advantage in the years to come.

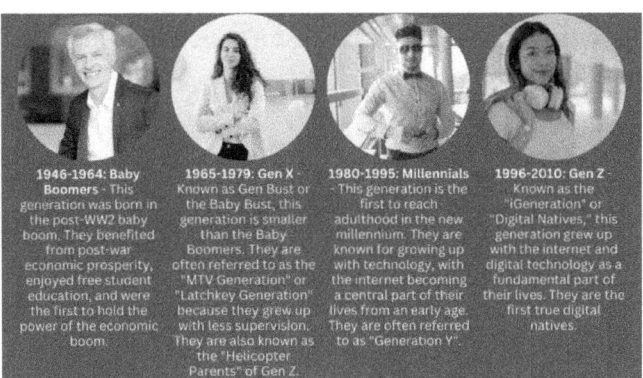

Picture 1.2. Comparison of Generations

In the workforce, Gen Z is looking for meaningful work that aligns with their values and provides opportunities for growth and development. They prioritize work-life balance and are more likely to seek out flexible work arrangements and remote work options. By understanding the demographic characteristics of Gen Z, companies can create job ads and recruitment strategies that resonate with this generation. Companies that offer meaningful work, flexible work arrangements, and prioritize social and environmental issues will be more successful in attracting and retaining Gen Z talent.

Employers who fail to adapt to the needs and expectations of Gen Z risk falling behind in the race for talent. Gen Z is known to prioritize purpose and personal growth in their careers over just a paycheck. This means that companies who can offer meaningful work and opportunities for development are more likely to attract and retain Gen Z employees. Moreover, Gen Z is the most diverse generation yet, and they value diversity and inclusion in the workplace. Companies that embrace diversity and create inclusive environments are more likely to attract and retain Gen Z talent.

Overall, Gen Z brings a fresh perspective and a unique set of skills to the table. Employers who can understand and adapt to their needs will be able to harness their potential and gain a competitive advantage in the workforce.

## I.2. The challenges of hiring Gen Z

Hiring Gen Z presents a unique set of challenges for employers. First and foremost, Gen Z is a highly discerning and tech-savvy generation that expects a seamless digital hiring experience. They expect companies to have a strong online presence and to be active on social media. Gen Z values transparency and authenticity in their interactions with employers. They expect companies to be upfront about their values, culture, and expectations. This means that companies need to be clear about their mission, vision, and purpose to attract Gen Z talent.

Expectations from Gen Z is for work-life balance and flexibility. They value a healthy work-life balance and are more likely to prioritize their mental health and well-being over their job. Companies that can offer flexible work arrangements and a supportive culture are more likely to attract and retain Gen Z employees. They are highly selective and discerning when it comes to job opportunities. They are not afraid to turn down job offers that don't align with their values or expectations. This means that companies need to have a strong employer brand and a compelling employee value proposition to attract and retain Gen Z talent.

In addition to the challenges mentioned above, companies also need to be aware that Gen Z has different communication preferences compared to previous generations. They prefer informal and personalized communication, and they tend to communicate through instant messaging apps and social media rather than email or phone calls. Gen Z values diversity and inclusion in the workplace. They expect companies to create inclusive environments that value and respect all employees regardless of their backgrounds. Companies that fail to promote diversity and inclusion risk losing out on Gen Z talent.

Another challenge in hiring Gen Z is that they tend to switch jobs more frequently compared to previous generations. This means that companies need to provide continuous learning and development opportunities to keep Gen Z employees engaged and motivated. Companies need to be aware that Gen Z is a socially conscious generation that values environmental and social responsibility. They expect companies to be transparent about their social and environmental impact and to actively work towards making a positive change in society.

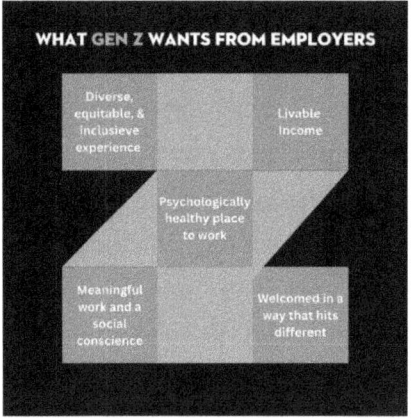

Picture 1.3. What Gen Z Wants from Employers

To overcome these challenges, companies need to create a culture of transparency, authenticity, and continuous learning. They need to embrace digital communication channels and promote diversity and inclusion in the workplace. Companies that can provide work-life balance, continuous learning and development opportunities, and promote social and environmental responsibility will be more successful in attracting and retaining Gen Z talent.

Overall, hiring Gen Z requires companies to adapt to their unique needs and expectations. Companies that can create a seamless digital hiring experience, offer work-life balance and flexibility, and have a strong employer brand will be more successful in hiring Gen Z talent.

## I.3. The benefits of hiring Gen Z

Hiring Gen Z can bring a range of benefits to companies. Gen Z is a diverse and dynamic generation that brings fresh perspectives, skills, and ideas to the workforce. Here are some of the key benefits of hiring Gen Z:

- **Adaptability**: Gen Z is the first generation to grow up in the digital age, which means they are highly adaptable and quick to learn new skills. They are

comfortable with technology and are often early adopters of new tools and software.
- **Innovation**: Gen Z is known for their creativity and innovation. They are not afraid to challenge the status quo and bring new ideas to the table. They have a unique perspective that can help companies innovate and stay ahead of the competition.
- **Diversity**: Gen Z is the most diverse generation yet, with a wide range of cultural, ethnic, and socioeconomic backgrounds. Hiring Gen Z can help companies build a more diverse and inclusive workforce, which can lead to better decision-making and improved performance.
- **Purpose-driven**: Gen Z is a purpose-driven generation that values meaningful work and personal growth. They are more likely to stay with a company that aligns with their values and provides opportunities for development and growth.
- **Digital savvy**: Gen Z is comfortable with digital tools and social media, which can help companies improve their online presence and engage with customers more effectively.

Overall, hiring Gen Z can bring a range of benefits to companies, from innovation and creativity to diversity and adaptability. Companies that can attract and retain Gen Z talent will be well-positioned to succeed in the years to come.

To attract and retain Gen Z talent, companies need to understand their unique needs and preferences. Here are some strategies that can help companies effectively recruit and retain Gen Z:

- **Embrace digital channels**: Gen Z is a digital-savvy generation that prefers to communicate through instant messaging apps and social media. Companies need to embrace digital channels to connect with Gen Z candidates and provide a seamless digital hiring experience.
- **Promote work-life balance and flexibility**: Gen Z values work-life balance and flexibility, which means companies need to provide flexible work arrangements and prioritize work-life balance. This can help companies attract and retain Gen Z talent, as well as improve employee satisfaction and productivity.
- **Create a strong employer brand**: Gen Z is highly selective when it comes to choosing an employer.

Companies need to create a strong employer brand that reflects their values, culture, and mission. This can help companies stand out from the competition and attract top Gen Z talent.

- **Provide continuous learning and development opportunities**: Gen Z values personal and professional development, which means companies need to provide continuous learning and development opportunities. This can include mentorship programs, training and development opportunities, and regular feedback and coaching.
- **Promote diversity and inclusion**: Gen Z values diversity and inclusion in the workplace. Companies need to promote diversity and inclusion in their recruitment and hiring practices, as well as create a culture that values and respects all employees.

By implementing these strategies, companies can attract and retain top Gen Z talent and create a dynamic and innovative workforce. In the next chapters, we will explore each of these strategies in more detail and provide practical tips and case studies to help companies effectively hire and retain Gen Z talent.

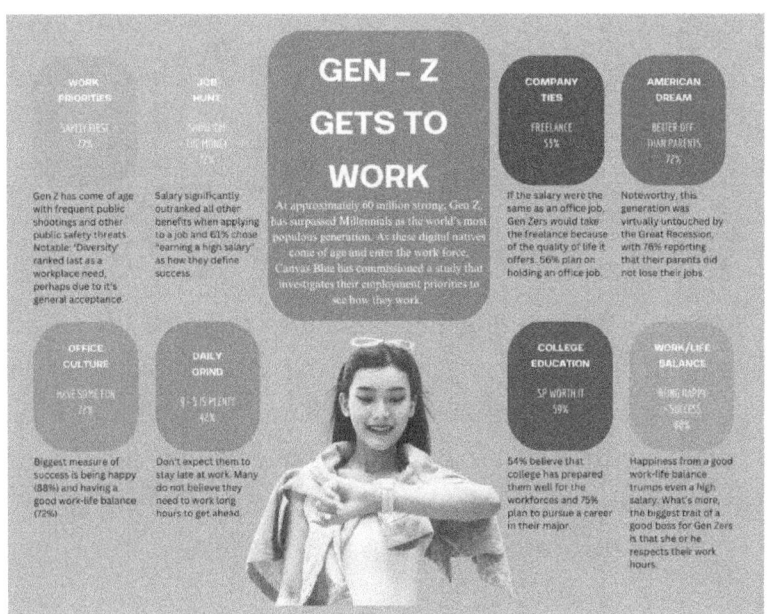

Picture 1.4. Gen Z in the Workplace

# II. Creating Job Ads that Attract Gen Z

Creating effective job ads is essential for attracting Gen Z talent. Gen Z has grown up in a digital world and is accustomed to scrolling through online content quickly. To capture their attention, job ads need to be clear, concise, and engaging. In this chapter, we will explore how to create job ads that resonate with Gen Z candidates.

## II.1. Understanding Gen Z's job search behavior

Gen Z's job search behavior is different from previous generations. They prefer to use digital channels to search for jobs and are more likely to apply for positions that align with their values and career goals. They are also more likely to research companies and read reviews from current and former employees before applying for a job. Their behavior is heavily influenced by their digital upbringing. They are comfortable with technology and prefer to use digital channels to search for jobs. Gen Z candidates are also more likely to apply for positions that align with their values and career goals.

Gen Z candidates are more likely to research companies and read reviews from current and former employees before applying for a job. They want to work for companies that share their values and have a positive reputation in the industry. Another important aspect of Gen Z's job search behavior is their preference for flexibility and work-life balance. They prioritize their personal lives and are looking for jobs that offer flexible schedules, remote work options, and other benefits that support work-life balance.

Understanding Gen Z's job search behavior is critical for creating job ads that resonate with this generation. Companies that can offer a seamless digital hiring experience, prioritize work-life balance, and have a strong employer brand will be more successful in attracting Gen Z talent.

Picture 2.1. Generation Z's Most Valuable Job Search Sources

## II.2. Writing job ads that resonate with Gen Z

To create job ads that resonate with Gen Z, companies need to focus on the following:

- **Highlighting company culture**: Gen Z values company culture and wants to work for companies that share their values. Job ads should highlight the company's mission, values, and culture to attract Gen Z candidates.
- **Being clear and concise**: Gen Z candidates have short attention spans and are more likely to skim job ads quickly. Companies need to be clear and concise in their job ads, highlighting the most important information at the beginning.

- **Offering competitive salaries and benefits**: Gen Z candidates are more likely to research salaries and benefits before applying for a job. Companies need to offer competitive salaries and benefits packages to attract top Gen Z talent.
- **Using inclusive language**: Gen Z is a diverse generation that values inclusion and diversity. Companies need to use inclusive language in their job ads to attract a wider range of candidates.
- **Providing information on career growth and development**: Gen Z values career growth and development. Companies need to provide information on opportunities for career growth and development in their job ads to attract top Gen Z talent.

## II.3. Using social media to promote job ads

Social media is a powerful tool for promoting job ads to Gen Z candidates. Gen Z spends a significant amount of time on social media, and companies can leverage this by sharing job ads on platforms like LinkedIn, Instagram, and Twitter.

To effectively promote job ads on social media, companies should consider the following:

- **Use visual content**: Gen Z responds well to visual content, so using images or videos in job ads can be more effective than text-only posts.
- **Use hashtags**: Using relevant hashtags in job ads can help increase their visibility on social media platforms. Companies can use industry-specific hashtags or those related to the job or company culture.
- **Share employee stories**: Sharing stories or testimonials from current employees can give job ads a personal touch and help attract Gen Z candidates who value company culture.
- **Use targeted advertising**: Social media platforms offer targeted advertising options that allow companies to reach specific demographics or interests. Companies can use this feature to target Gen Z candidates who are most likely to be interested in the job.

By using social media to promote job ads, companies can reach a wider audience and attract top Gen Z talent. It's important to use visual content, relevant hashtags, employee stories, and targeted advertising to make job ads stand out on social media platforms. Also, by understanding Gen Z's job search behavior and creating job ads that resonate with their values and preferences, companies can attract top Gen Z talent and build a strong and diverse workforce. In the next chapter, we will explore how to attract Gen Z candidates through effective employer branding strategies.

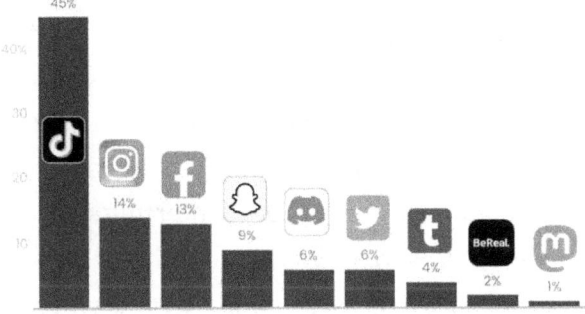

Picture 2.2. Most talk about social media by Gen Z between February 2022 – February 2023

## II.4. How to Create Job Ads that Speak to Gen Z

Creating job ads that speak to Gen Z candidates requires a deep understanding of their values, interests, and communication preferences. Here are some tips for creating job ads that resonate with Gen Z:

- **Focus on impact**: Gen Z candidates want to make a difference in the world, and they are attracted to roles that offer meaningful work and the opportunity to have an impact. Highlight the ways in which the role will contribute to a larger mission or social or environmental cause.
- **Emphasize growth and development**: Gen Z candidates are eager to learn and grow in their careers. Highlight opportunities for professional development, such as training programs or mentorship opportunities.
- **Use inclusive language**: Gen Z is a diverse generation, and they value inclusivity and diversity in the workplace. Use inclusive language in job ads, and highlight the ways in which the company values

diversity and is committed to creating an inclusive work environment.
- **Highlight unique benefits**: Gen Z candidates are looking for more than just a paycheck. Highlight unique benefits such as flexible work arrangements, opportunities for remote work, or wellness programs.
- **Use visuals**: Gen Z is a highly visual generation, and they respond well to images and videos. Incorporate visuals into job ads to make them more engaging and memorable.

By following these tips, companies can create job ads that speak to Gen Z candidates and help to attract top talent.

Picture 2.3. Example of Job Ads for Gen Z

# III. Attracting Gen Z Candidates

Attracting Gen Z candidates requires more than just creating compelling job ads. Companies must also have a strong employer brand and a presence on the channels and platforms that Gen Z candidates are using for job search. Here are some strategies for attracting Gen Z candidates.

## III.1. Build a Strong Employer Brand

In order to attract Gen Z candidates, it is important for companies to build a strong employer brand. A strong employer brand can help a company stand out in a crowded job market and attract top talent. Gen Z candidates, in particular, value transparency, authenticity, and social responsibility, so companies that prioritize these values in their employer brand are more likely to resonate with Gen Z candidates.

To build a strong employer brand for Gen Z, companies can start by creating a compelling employee value proposition (EVP) that clearly communicates the company's values, culture, and mission. This can be done through company website content, social media, and employee testimonials. Companies can also leverage social media to showcase their culture and values and engage with potential candidates. This can include sharing behind the scenes photos and videos, highlighting employee achievements and recognition, and responding to candidate inquiries and comments.

Another important aspect of building a strong employer brand for Gen Z is being transparent and authentic. This means being honest about the company's successes and challenges, as well as its commitment to social and environmental responsibility. Gen Z candidates value companies that are open and transparent, and are more likely to be attracted to companies that are genuine and authentic.

Overall, building a strong employer brand is essential for attracting and retaining Gen Z talent. By communicating a clear and compelling EVP, leveraging social media, and being transparent and authentic, companies can create an employer brand that resonates with Gen Z candidates and positions themselves for success in the years to come.

## III.2. Use Social Media

Gen Z candidates are highly active on social media, and companies can use these platforms to attract top talent. This can include promoting job openings, showcasing company culture, and highlighting employee stories. Companies should aim to be authentic and engaging on social media, using language and visuals that resonate with Gen Z. Social media is a powerful tool for attracting Gen Z candidates and building a strong employer brand. Gen Z candidates are highly engaged on social media platforms, and are more likely to apply to companies that have a strong social media presence.

To use social media effectively in attracting Gen Z candidates, companies should start by identifying the platforms that are most popular among Gen Z, such as Instagram, TikTok, and Snapchat. Companies can then create a social media strategy that aligns with their employer brand and showcases their culture, values, and job opportunities. One effective strategy is to use employee-generated content on social media, such as photos and videos of employees at work or participating in company events. This type of content is more authentic and engaging than branded content, and can help to showcase the company's culture and values.

Another strategy is to leverage social media influencers who are popular among Gen Z. By partnering with influencers who align with the company's values and mission, companies can reach a wider audience and build credibility with potential candidates. Social media can also be used to promote job opportunities and engage with potential candidates. Companies can use social media ads to target specific demographics and promote job openings, and can also use direct messaging to answer candidate questions and build relationships.

Overall, social media is a powerful tool for attracting Gen Z candidates and building a strong employer brand. By leveraging employee-generated content, influencers, and targeted ads, companies can reach a wider audience and position themselves as an employer of choice for Gen Z talent.

Picture 3.1. Social Media

## III.3. Offer Flexibility and Work-Life Balance

Gen Z candidates value flexibility and work-life balance, and companies that offer these benefits will be more attractive to Gen Z talent. This can include offering remote work options, flexible schedules, and generous paid time off policies. Flexibility and work-life balance are top priorities for Gen Z candidates when considering job opportunities. Offering flexible work arrangements, such as remote work and flexible hours, can help companies attract and retain top Gen Z talent.

To offer flexibility and work-life balance, companies should start by understanding the needs and preferences of Gen Z candidates. This generation values work-life balance, and often seeks opportunities that allow them to pursue their passions and interests outside of work. One effective strategy is to offer flexible work arrangements that allow employees to work from home or adjust their schedules as needed. Companies can also offer generous vacation and PTO policies, and encourage employees to take time off to recharge and pursue their interests outside of work. In addition to offering flexible work arrangements, companies can also prioritize employee wellness by offering health and wellness benefits, such as gym memberships, mental health resources, and healthy snack options in the workplace.

Overall, offering flexibility and work-life balance is essential for attracting and retaining top Gen Z talent. By understanding the needs and preferences of this generation and prioritizing employee wellness, companies can position themselves as an employer of choice for Gen Z candidates.

## III.4. Prioritize Social and Environmental Issues

Gen Z is a socially conscious generation, and they are more likely to be attracted to companies that prioritize social and environmental issues. Companies should highlight their commitment to sustainability, diversity, and social responsibility in their employer branding efforts. By building a strong employer brand, using social media effectively, offering flexibility and work-life balance, and prioritizing social and environmental issues, companies can attract top Gen Z talent and position themselves for success in the years to come. Prioritizing social and environmental issues is not only important for attracting Gen Z candidates, but also for appealing to customers and clients who are increasingly focused on social responsibility and sustainability. By prioritizing these issues, companies can position themselves as leaders in their industries and build a positive reputation among customers and stakeholders.

Companies can also consider offering opportunities for professional development and growth, providing competitive salaries and benefits packages, and creating a positive and inclusive work environment. Gen Z candidates value these aspects of a job and are more likely to be attracted to companies that prioritize them. They can leverage technology to streamline their hiring process and create a seamless candidate experience. This can include using applicant tracking systems, video interviews, and online assessments. These tools not only make the hiring process more efficient but also align with Gen Z's preference for technology-driven solutions.

By implementing these strategies, companies can attract and retain Gen Z talent and create a diverse and innovative workforce that is well-equipped to succeed in the rapidly evolving business landscape.

Picture 3.2. ASEAN Gen Z to work for Environmentally Responsible Organizations

## III.5. The importance of mobile optimization

Mobile optimization is critical when it comes to attracting and engaging Gen Z candidates. This demographic primarily uses their smartphones to access the internet, social media, and job boards, making it essential for companies to ensure that their online presence is optimized for mobile devices. When it comes to job postings, companies should ensure that their career website and job boards are optimized for mobile devices. This includes using a responsive design that adapts to different screen sizes and ensuring that the application process is mobile-friendly.

Companies should also consider using mobile recruiting apps to streamline the hiring process and make it easier for candidates to apply on-the-go. These apps can also provide valuable insights into candidate behavior and help companies to more effectively reach and engage with top talent in the Gen Z demographic.

Overall, by prioritizing mobile optimization in their recruiting efforts, companies can ensure that they are able to effectively connect with and engage Gen Z candidates, who rely heavily on their smartphones for their job search and online activities.

This can ultimately lead to a stronger employer brand and better recruitment outcomes for companies looking to attract and retain top Gen Z talent. By embracing mobile optimization and providing a seamless and user-friendly mobile experience, companies can demonstrate that they understand the needs and preferences of this demographic and are committed to providing a modern and innovative work environment.

## III.6. Using video and visual content to attract Gen Z

Gen Z is a highly visual generation that values authentic and engaging content. Using video and visual content can be an effective way to attract Gen Z candidates and communicate the unique aspects of your company culture and values. For example, creating short videos that showcase your workplace, team members, and company mission can be a powerful way to give Gen Z candidates a glimpse into what it would be like to work for your organization. Visuals such as infographics, memes, and other shareable content can also be used to create a more dynamic and engaging social media presence that resonates with Gen Z's preferences for visual and interactive content.

By using video and visual content, companies can stand out from the competition and better connect with Gen Z candidates.

Using video and visual content can also help to retain and engage this generation once they are hired. Providing regular updates and behind-the-scenes glimpses of company initiatives and events can keep Gen Z employees connected and engaged with their work and the organization as a whole. Additionally, using visual tools such as interactive training modules and gamified learning experiences can help to make learning and development more engaging and effective for Gen Z employees. By incorporating video and visual content into various aspects of the employee experience, companies can better meet the needs and preferences of Gen Z and build a more engaged and committed workforce.

Picture 3.3. Job Advertisement through Youtube

# IV. Selecting Gen Z Candidates

Selecting the right Gen Z candidate requires a careful and thorough evaluation process. Companies should start by reviewing resumes and cover letters for relevant experience and skills, and then move on to conducting behavioral-based interviews to assess candidates' problem-solving, communication, and teamwork abilities. It's also important to involve current employees in the interview process to get a sense of how candidates might fit within the company culture. Using assessments and other selection tools can provide additional insights into candidates' strengths and weaknesses, helping companies make more informed hiring decisions.

## IV.1. Identifying Key Skills and Competencies

As companies seek to select the best Gen Z candidates for their workforce, it is important to identify the key skills and competencies that are essential for this generation. Some of the top skills and competencies that Gen Z employees possess include strong digital literacy, adaptability, creativity, teamwork, and a passion for social and environmental issues. Companies should focus on evaluating these skills and competencies during the selection process to ensure that they are hiring candidates who are well-suited to the demands of the modern workplace. By identifying these key skills and competencies, companies can better understand what they should be looking for in potential Gen Z hires and make more informed hiring decisions.

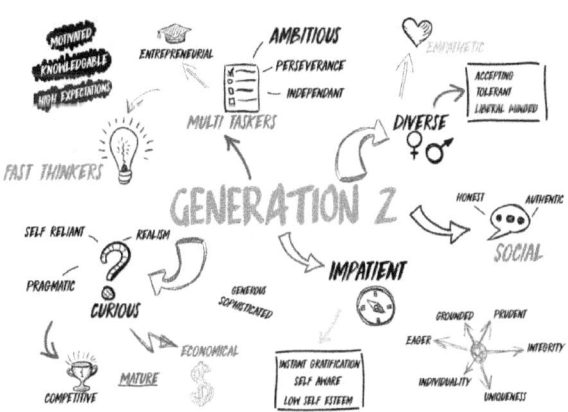

Picture 4.1. Gen Z Characteristics

Understanding the skills and competencies that are essential for Gen Z employees can help companies tailor their job descriptions and interview questions to better assess candidates' qualifications. This can lead to more successful hiring outcomes and a stronger workforce overall.

## IV.2. Resumes and Cover Letters

When reviewing resumes and cover letters for Gen Z candidates, it's important to look beyond traditional markers of experience and education. Many Gen Z candidates may have gained valuable skills and experience through internships, volunteer work, or extracurricular activities. Look for evidence of initiative, leadership, and problem-solving skills, as well as a demonstrated passion for the industry or field. Additionally, pay attention to the candidate's communication skills, both written and verbal, as clear and effective communication is essential for success in any role. Finally, keep an eye out for any unique or creative experiences or achievements that demonstrate the candidate's individuality and potential to bring new perspectives and ideas to the company.

Additionally, it's important to look for transferable skills, such as communication, problem-solving, and adaptability, as many Gen Z candidates may not have extensive work experience. When reviewing cover letters, pay attention to the candidate's writing style and ability to clearly articulate their qualifications and interest in the role. It can also be helpful to look for any alignment between the candidate's values and the company's mission and culture. Ultimately, a strong resume and cover letter should showcase the candidate's potential to thrive in the role and contribute to the company's success.

## IV.3. Assessments and Tests

There are several types of assessments and tests that can be used to evaluate Gen Z candidates. One common type is cognitive ability tests, which measure a candidate's ability to learn, solve problems, and adapt to new situations. Personality tests can also be useful in evaluating candidates' traits and behaviors, such as their work style, communication skills, and emotional intelligence. Additionally, situational judgment tests can assess how candidates respond to hypothetical scenarios they may encounter in the workplace. These assessments can provide valuable insights into a candidate's potential fit with the company culture and job requirements. However, it is important to use these assessments in conjunction with other hiring methods and not rely solely on them.

While assessments and tests can provide valuable insights into a candidate's skills and abilities, they should not be the sole determinant of whether or not a candidate is the right fit for a company. Other factors, such as the candidate's experience, cultural fit, and soft skills, should also be taken into consideration when making a hiring decision. It is important to use a combination of methods to ensure that the candidate is the best fit for the role and the company's culture.

## IV.4. Behavioral Interviews

Behavioral interviews are a valuable tool for assessing Gen Z candidates' competencies and skills. When conducting behavioral interviews, it's essential to ask questions that are relevant to the specific role and focus on the candidate's past experiences and behaviors. Questions should be open-ended, allowing candidates to provide detailed responses, and should provide opportunities for candidates to showcase their problem-solving and communication skills. It's also important to tailor the interview process to Gen Z candidates by incorporating technology and providing a positive and engaging experience. This can include using video interviews or gamification techniques to make the process more interactive and enjoyable. By conducting effective behavioral interviews, companies can better evaluate Gen Z candidates and make informed hiring decisions.

## IV.5. Diversity and Inclusion in Selection

Diversity and inclusion are essential components of any successful hiring process, and this is particularly true when it comes to Gen Z candidates. Companies should strive to create a diverse and inclusive workplace that values and respects people from all backgrounds, experiences, and identities. To ensure that the selection process is inclusive, companies should take steps to eliminate bias in their hiring practices and actively seek out a diverse pool of candidates. This can include posting job ads on platforms that are popular with underrepresented groups, using gender-neutral language in job descriptions, and training hiring managers on how to conduct inclusive interviews. By prioritizing diversity and inclusion in the selection process, companies can attract and retain top Gen Z talent and create a more innovative and dynamic workplace.

## IV.6. Decision-Making and Selection

When it comes to making a final decision and selecting the best Gen Z candidate for the role, it's important to consider all aspects of the candidate's application and interview process. One effective strategy is to create a scoring system that assigns points to each candidate based on their qualifications, experience, and interview performance. This can help eliminate any unconscious biases and ensure that the best candidate is selected based on objective criteria. It's also important to involve multiple stakeholders in the decision-making process, including team members who will be working closely with the new hire. Finally, make sure to communicate clearly and promptly with all candidates, providing feedback and thanking them for their time and interest in the position.

It is important to involve multiple stakeholders in the decision-making process to ensure that different perspectives are taken into account. Companies should also consider offering the selected Gen Z candidate a personalized onboarding experience that meets their unique needs and preferences. Finally, it is crucial to maintain a positive employer brand and reputation throughout the selection process, as this can impact the perception of the company among not only the selected candidate but also all other applicants and potential future hires.

## IV.7. Legal Considerations in Selection

When selecting Gen Z candidates, it is important for companies to be aware of and comply with legal considerations. These include avoiding discrimination based on protected characteristics such as age, gender, race, and disability, as well as ensuring compliance with relevant laws and regulations such as the Americans with Disabilities Act (ADA) and the Fair Labor Standards Act (FLSA). Companies should also be careful to avoid asking inappropriate or illegal questions during the hiring process, such as questions about a candidate's marital status or pregnancy status. By being aware of these legal considerations and taking steps to ensure compliance, companies can minimize the risk of legal issues arising during the selection process.

In Indonesia, there are several legal considerations that companies must keep in mind when selecting Gen Z candidates. Firstly, it is important to avoid discrimination on the basis of race, religion, gender, ethnicity, or other protected characteristics. Employers must also comply with the labor laws and regulations, such as the Manpower Law, which sets out the minimum age for employment and requirements for working hours, overtime, and benefits. Companies must ensure that they are not engaging in any unlawful practices, such as forcing candidates to provide personal information beyond what is necessary for the selection process. Additionally, companies should also ensure that they have a clear and transparent selection process that is free from any bias or prejudice.

## IV.8. The importance of skills and cultural fit

Skills and cultural fit are both important factors to consider when selecting Gen Z candidates. While having the necessary skills and experience is essential for the role, it is also important to consider how the candidate's personality, values, and working style align with the company's culture. A candidate who is a good cultural fit is more likely to be engaged and productive in their role, and may also contribute to a positive and collaborative work environment. Therefore, it is important to assess both skills and cultural fit when making hiring decisions.

Assessing both skills and cultural fit is crucial in making hiring decisions for Gen Z candidates. While having the necessary skills and qualifications is important, cultural fit plays a significant role in determining a candidate's success in the company. Cultural fit refers to how well a candidate's values, beliefs, and work style align with the company's culture and values. By hiring candidates who fit well with the company culture, it increases the likelihood of job satisfaction and overall job performance, leading to increased productivity and retention rates.

To assess skills, companies can use a combination of methods, such as reviewing resumes, conducting skills assessments and tests, and asking behavioral interview questions tailored to the specific skills required for the role. To assess cultural fit, companies can use various methods, such as evaluating the candidate's values, work style, and communication skills, as well as asking situational interview questions to gauge how the candidate would handle certain workplace scenarios. Additionally, conducting reference checks and background screenings can provide further insights into a candidate's skills and cultural fit. By utilizing these methods, companies can make informed hiring decisions and select the best Gen Z candidate for the role.

## IV.9. The Role of Technology in Candidate Selection

Technology has revolutionized the way companies attract, evaluate, and select candidates, particularly with the emergence of artificial intelligence (AI) and machine learning (ML) tools. These technologies can help companies streamline their recruitment processes, improve the candidate experience, and make more data-driven hiring decisions. For example, AI and ML algorithms can analyze resumes, assess candidate fit, and even conduct initial interviews using chatbots. However, it is important to use these technologies ethically and transparently, and to ensure that human oversight and judgment is still integrated into the selection process.

Additionally, it is crucial for companies to ensure that their selection technologies are free from bias and are accessible to all candidates, including those with disabilities. Using technology in candidate selection can streamline the process, improve efficiency, and increase the likelihood of finding the best Gen Z candidates for the role. However, it should not replace the value of personal interaction and human judgment in the hiring process.

# V. Interview Guide for Hiring Gen Z

The interview guide for hiring Gen Z includes questions that focus on their values, goals, experience, and skills to help companies assess their cultural fit and potential for success in the role.

- Begin by asking the candidate to tell you about themselves, their background, and their experiences. This can help you get a better understanding of who they are and what they can bring to the company.
- Ask the candidate about their career goals and aspirations. This will help you determine whether they are a good fit for the role and the company.
- Inquire about their preferred work style and environment. Gen Z values flexibility and work-life balance, so it is important to make sure the company can accommodate their needs.

- Ask about their experience with technology and social media. Gen Z is known for their proficiency with technology, so this can give you a better idea of their skills and how they can contribute to the company's digital presence.
- Inquire about their experience working in teams and collaborating with others. Gen Z is known for their collaborative and inclusive approach to work, so it is important to make sure they can work well with others.
- Ask the candidate about any experiences or projects that demonstrate their creativity or problem-solving skills. This can help you evaluate their potential to bring new ideas and perspectives to the company.
- Inquire about the candidate's understanding and alignment with the company's values and mission. Gen Z is known for their desire to work for companies that prioritize social and environmental issues, so it is important to make sure the company's values align with the candidate's.
- Ask the candidate about any challenges they have faced and how they overcame them. This can help you evaluate their resilience and ability to adapt to change.

- Inquire about the candidate's preferred methods of feedback and communication. Gen Z values regular feedback and open communication, so it is important to make sure the company can provide this.
- End the interview by asking if the candidate has any questions or concerns about the role or the company. This can help you address any potential issues and ensure the candidate has a clear understanding of the position and the company.

## V.1. The importance of structured interviews

Structured interviews are an essential part of the hiring process for Gen Z candidates as they can help to assess the candidate's skills, cultural fit, and potential for success in the role, while reducing bias and increasing the chances of finding the best fit for the job.

## V.2. How to design a structured interview process

When designing a structured interview process for Gen Z candidates, it's important to establish a set of consistent and relevant questions, as well as a standardized scoring system to evaluate responses. Additionally, it's important to provide clear instructions and training to interviewers to ensure consistency and reduce the risk of bias.

When designing a structured interview process for Gen Z candidates, companies should start by clearly defining the job requirements and identifying the key skills and competencies necessary for success in the role. Then, they can develop a list of questions that are designed to evaluate these skills and competencies, as well as the candidate's experience and qualifications. The questions should be standardized and asked in the same order to all candidates, and the interviewers should have a clear rubric for evaluating the responses. Additionally, companies should consider including behavioral questions that assess how the candidate has handled relevant situations in the past.

Incorporating behavioral questions is a crucial aspect of designing a structured interview process for Gen Z candidates. Behavioral questions help in assessing how a candidate has handled real-life situations in the past and whether they possess the required skills and competencies for the job. It is also essential to design a rating scale to evaluate the responses consistently across all candidates. Companies should also consider having multiple interviewers and using technology to streamline the interview process, such as recording the interviews for later evaluation.

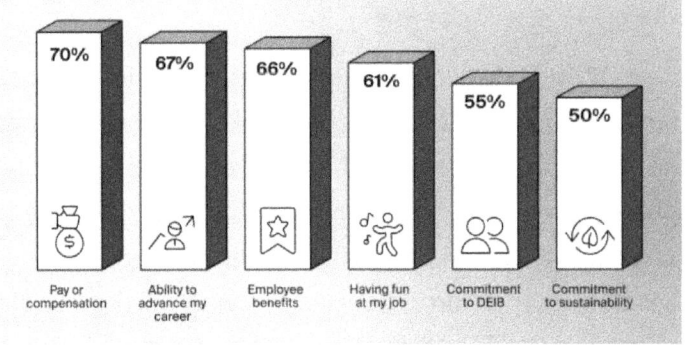

Picture 5.1. Job Factors Important for Gen Z

## V.3. Tips for conducting effective interviews with Gen Z candidates

When conducting interviews with Gen Z candidates, it is important to create a comfortable and inclusive environment where they feel valued and heard. Some tips for conducting effective interviews include being transparent about the role and company culture, asking open-ended questions to encourage conversation, and actively listening to the candidate's responses. Additionally, using visual aids and technology can help to engage Gen Z candidates and better assess their skills and potential fit for the role. Finally, providing clear feedback and next steps at the end of the interview can help to build a positive candidate experience and reflect well on the company.

Additionally, it is important to establish a comfortable and conversational tone during the interview, as well as actively listen to the candidate's responses and ask follow-up questions. Avoiding assumptions and stereotypes, showing interest in the candidate's experiences and perspectives, and being transparent about the company culture and expectations can also help to engage and attract top Gen Z talent. Finally, providing clear feedback and next steps at the end of the interview can help to build a positive candidate experience and reflect well on the company.

# VI. Making Job Offers to Gen Z

After identifying and assessing potential Gen Z candidates, the next step is to make a job offer. Companies need to ensure that they make an attractive offer that reflects the candidate's market value and meets their expectations. This is particularly important with Gen Z, as they are known for prioritizing work-life balance and meaningful work experiences. The job offer should include a competitive salary, benefits, and opportunities for growth and development. It's also important to provide a clear and concise job description, including the role's responsibilities and expectations. Lastly, companies should be transparent and communicative throughout the offer process, keeping the candidate informed of the next steps and providing feedback when necessary.

It is important for companies to be flexible and open to negotiation, as Gen Z candidates may prioritize factors such as work-life balance and opportunities for growth and development. Offering competitive compensation packages and benefits can also help to attract top Gen Z talent and retain employees in the long term. By making job offers that meet the needs and expectations of Gen Z candidates, companies can build a strong employer brand and position themselves as an attractive and supportive workplace.

## Job offers negotiation with Gen Z

When negotiating job offers with Gen Z candidates, it is important to understand their priorities and motivations. Many Gen Z candidates prioritize flexibility and work-life balance, so companies may want to consider offering remote work options or flexible schedules. Additionally, Gen Z candidates may value opportunities for growth and development, so companies should be prepared to discuss potential career paths and training opportunities. It is also important to be transparent about compensation and benefits, as Gen Z candidates tend to prioritize fair compensation and comprehensive benefits packages. Overall, companies should approach job offer negotiations with Gen Z candidates in a collaborative and transparent manner, prioritizing open communication and mutual understanding.

Additionally, companies should be prepared to offer competitive and personalized compensation packages, as Gen Z candidates may place a high value on salary and benefits. It is also important to be flexible and open to negotiation, as Gen Z candidates may have different priorities and preferences when it comes to job offers. Companies should also consider the potential for offering non-monetary benefits, such as flexible work arrangements or opportunities for professional development, which can be particularly attractive to Gen Z candidates. Overall, a collaborative and flexible approach to job offer negotiation can help to build a positive relationship with Gen Z candidates and increase the likelihood of a successful hiring outcome.

## VI.1. The importance of transparent communication

Transparent communication is essential when making job offers to Gen Z candidates. Companies should provide all relevant information about the role, compensation, benefits, and career growth opportunities to ensure that the candidate has a clear understanding of what the position entails.

An example of transparent communication during job offer negotiation could be sharing the salary range for the position upfront and explaining the factors that influenced the final offer. Additionally, providing a clear explanation of the benefits package and any potential opportunities for growth and development within the company can help to establish trust and build a positive relationship with the candidate.

An example of not transparent communication during a job offer negotiation with a Gen Z candidate might be if the company makes promises or offers that they cannot fulfill, such as promising a certain salary or benefits package but not delivering on those promises after the candidate accepts the job offer.

## VI.2. How to create a compelling job offer

To create a compelling job offer for Gen Z candidates, companies should consider including a competitive salary and benefits package, opportunities for professional development and growth, a positive company culture and work-life balance, and a clear description of the job responsibilities and expectations. It is also important to highlight any unique aspects of the company or role that may appeal to Gen Z's desire for purpose and impact.

When offering jobs to Gen Z, companies should avoid making assumptions based on stereotypes, offering inadequate compensation or benefits, using inflexible work arrangements, and failing to prioritize diversity and inclusion in the workplace. It is also important to avoid making promises that cannot be kept and to be transparent about the role and expectations.

## VI.3. Negotiating with Gen Z candidates

When negotiating with Gen Z candidates, companies should be open to discussing and considering their preferences and needs. This can include flexible work arrangements, career development opportunities, and a fair salary package. It is important to approach negotiations with a willingness to collaborate and find a mutually beneficial solution. Additionally, it is important to be transparent and honest throughout the negotiation process, setting clear expectations and discussing any potential limitations or constraints.

Companies should be flexible and open to compromise, understanding that Gen Z candidates may prioritize work-life balance, growth opportunities, and company culture over traditional benefits like salary and healthcare. By finding creative solutions and meeting the needs of both parties, companies can build a positive and long-lasting relationship with their Gen Z hires.

# VII. Case Studies and Examples of hiring Gen z candidates

The case studies and examples of hiring Gen Z candidates highlight the importance of understanding their unique characteristics and preferences, implementing innovative recruitment strategies, prioritizing diversity and inclusion, and providing a positive candidate experience throughout the hiring process.

A few examples of companies successfully hiring Gen Z candidates:

- **Deloitte**: Deloitte launched a "Millennial Impact Report" to better understand the values and goals of the millennial and Gen Z workforce. The report showed that these generations prioritize a sense of purpose and a positive work-life balance. In response, Deloitte created a recruitment process

that emphasizes these values, including promoting volunteer opportunities and flexible work arrangements.
- **IBM**: IBM has implemented a "New Collar" hiring strategy that focuses on skills and potential rather than traditional degree requirements. This strategy has allowed IBM to tap into a diverse pool of talent, including many Gen Z candidates, who may not have pursued traditional four-year degrees.
- **LinkedIn**: LinkedIn has shifted its hiring focus to prioritize soft skills such as communication and collaboration, which are highly valued by Gen Z. The company also uses artificial intelligence and machine learning tools to screen for potential bias in job descriptions and candidate assessments.
- **Marriott International**: Marriott International has developed a comprehensive Gen Z hiring program called "Voyage" that includes internships, mentorship, and career development opportunities. The program emphasizes building a strong employer brand and fostering a sense of community among employees.
- **PwC**: PwC has launched a "Flexibility2 Talent Network" that provides flexible work arrangements for employees, including Gen Z candidates who value

work-life balance. The company also uses virtual reality technology to provide a more immersive and engaging recruitment experience for candidates.
- These examples demonstrate the importance of understanding and adapting to the needs and values of Gen Z candidates in order to attract and retain top talent.

## VII.1. A case study on gen z hiring in south-east asia

Company X, a multinational technology firm with operations in Southeast Asia, noticed a gap in their workforce in terms of attracting and retaining Gen Z talent. The company decided to revamp their recruitment strategy by prioritizing digital channels, using social media to advertise job vacancies and actively engaging with potential candidates online.

To attract Gen Z candidates, Company X also revised their employee value proposition (EVP) to emphasize work-life balance, career development opportunities, and flexible work arrangements. Additionally, the company restructured their interview process to include behavioral questions that assess a candidate's values and motivations, and to better gauge cultural fit with the company's mission and vision.

As a result of these changes, Company X saw an increase in Gen Z candidates applying for positions, and an improvement in their retention rates for this demographic. The company also reported an increase in overall employee satisfaction and productivity due to the more diverse and dynamic workforce.

### Conclusion of gen z hiring case study

As evidenced by the case studies presented, hiring Gen Z candidates requires a strategic and intentional approach that prioritizes flexibility, inclusivity, and a commitment to technology and innovation. By adapting recruitment strategies and utilizing new technologies, companies can attract and retain top Gen Z talent and create a more dynamic and innovative workplace.

## VII.2. Case studies of companies that have effectively hired and retained Gen Z employees

One example of a company that has effectively hired and retained Gen Z employees is Airbnb. The company has implemented a number of strategies to attract and retain young talent, including a strong emphasis on diversity and inclusion, as well as offering a range of unique employee benefits, such as travel credits and sabbaticals.

Another example is Cisco, which has focused on creating a company culture that values collaboration and innovation, while also providing opportunities for career development and growth. The company has also implemented a number of flexible work arrangements, such as remote work options and flexible schedules, which have helped to attract and retain Gen Z employees who value work-life balance.

Sephora has implemented a number of innovative recruitment strategies, such as using social media to engage with potential candidates and creating targeted advertising campaigns to reach young talent. The company has also focused on creating a supportive and inclusive work environment, with a range of employee resource groups and development programs to help young employees grow and succeed within the company.

Picture 7.1. AirBnB, IBM, Sephora

**Detail case study of gen z hiring in Airbnb**

Airbnb is a company that has placed a strong emphasis on hiring and retaining Gen Z employees. One of the ways in which they have been successful in doing so is by fostering a culture of diversity and inclusion within their organization.

To attract and retain Gen Z talent, Airbnb has implemented a number of strategies. First, they have emphasized the importance of a flexible and accommodating work environment, offering benefits such as unlimited vacation time, remote work opportunities, and comprehensive healthcare coverage.

Airbnb has also made a concerted effort to build a diverse and inclusive workplace culture. They have established employee resource groups that focus on diversity and inclusion, and have implemented a number of programs designed to attract and retain underrepresented talent.

In addition to these initiatives, Airbnb has also made an effort to use technology to streamline their recruitment and selection processes. They have implemented a variety of tools, including video interviews and online assessments, to help identify top candidates and make informed hiring decisions.

Overall, these strategies have helped Airbnb to effectively attract and retain Gen Z employees, and have contributed to their success as a company. By prioritizing flexibility, diversity, and technology, Airbnb has been able to build a strong and talented workforce that is well-suited to the challenges of the modern business environment.

# VIII. Conclusion

***Recap of key takeaways:***

- Understanding the characteristics and values of Gen Z is important when developing recruitment strategies and selecting candidates.
- Companies should prioritize creating an inclusive and diverse workplace culture to attract and retain Gen Z employees.
- Utilizing technology in the recruitment process can be effective, but it's important to use it ethically and transparently and to integrate human oversight.
- Structured interviews and behavioral questions can help to reduce bias and increase the chances of finding the best fit for the role.
- Communication and transparency are key when negotiating job offers with Gen Z candidates.
- Case studies and examples of successful Gen Z recruitment and retention strategies can provide insights and inspiration for companies.

### *Final thoughts on hiring Gen Z*

In conclusion, hiring Gen Z requires a unique approach that is tailored to their specific characteristics, preferences, and values. By understanding their expectations and motivations, companies can develop effective recruitment and selection strategies that attract and retain top Gen Z talent. This involves utilizing a combination of traditional and innovative recruitment methods, incorporating technology and social media, emphasizing cultural fit, and providing a positive candidate experience. Moreover, it is crucial to create a supportive and inclusive work environment that aligns with Gen Z's values of diversity, equity, and social responsibility.

Moving forward, companies that are successful in hiring and retaining Gen Z will be the ones that adapt to the changing workforce and prioritize the needs and preferences of this new generation. This will require ongoing efforts to stay informed about the latest trends and preferences of Gen Z, and to be flexible and responsive in adjusting recruitment and retention strategies accordingly. Companies that can effectively tap into the potential of Gen Z will gain a competitive advantage in the marketplace, as they will have access to a highly skilled and motivated talent pool that can drive innovation and growth.

Overall, hiring Gen Z is not only an opportunity for companies to fill their talent pipeline with highly skilled and diverse individuals, but also a chance to shape the future of work and to create a more inclusive and equitable workplace culture. By recognizing the unique strengths and values of Gen Z, and by adapting recruitment and retention strategies to meet their needs and preferences, companies can attract and retain the best Gen Z talent and build a workforce that is prepared for the challenges and opportunities of the 21st century.

# References

1. Smith, J. D. (2023). Gen Z: The Culture, Beliefs and Motivations Shaping the Next Generation. New York, NY: Penguin Random House.
2. Twenge, J. M. (2017). Generation Z Unfiltered: Facing Nine Hidden Challenges of the Most Anxious Population. HarperCollins.
3. Tapscott, D., & Williams, M. (2017). Zconomy: How Gen Z Will Change the Future of Business—and What to Do About It. Portfolio.
4. Nishizaki, S., & DellaNeve, J. (2021). Working with Gen Z: A Handbook to Recruit, Retain, and Reimagine the Future Workforce after COVID-19. Wiley.
5. Stillman, D. (2017). Gen Z @ Work: How the Next Generation Is Transforming the Workplace. HarperCollins.
6. Flippin, C. S. (2017). Generation Z in the Workplace: Helping the Newest Generation in the Workforce Build Successful Working Relationships and Career Paths. Routledge.
7. Deloitte Global 2024 Gen Z and Millennial Survey (2024). Deloitte Touche Tohmatsu Limited

www.ingramcontent.com/pod-product-compliance
Lightning Source LLC
Chambersburg PA
CBHW070409230526
45471CB00006B/2717